LIFE ON ALL FRONTS

Women in the First World War

Gill Thomas

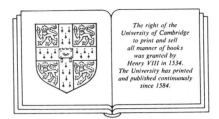

Published by the Press Syndicate of the University of Cambridge
The Pitt Building, Trumpington Street, Cambridge CB2 1RP
40 West 20th Street, New York, NY 10011, USA
10 Stamford Road, Oakleigh, Melbourne 3166, Australia

First published 1989

Printed in Great Britain at the University Press, Cambridge

British Library cataloguing in publication data
Thomas, Gill, 1961–
   Life on all fronts : women in the First
  World War – (Women in history)
  1. World War 1. Role of women.
  I. Title   II. Series
  940.3′15′042

ISBN 0 521 34841 2

VN

Library of Congress cataloguing in publication data

Thomas, Gill, 1961–
   Life on all fronts : Women in the First World War /
  Gill Thomas. (Women in history)
  1. World War, 1914–1918 – Women – Juvenile litera
  I. Title.
II. Series.
D639.W7T46 1989
940.3′15′03042–dc 19   88–20378 CIP AC

Acknowledgements

My thanks to all those who have helped in the writing of this book, especially Anna Hiddleston, R. Vasant Kumar, Sue Millar, Suzanne Raitt, Don Stubbs, Alison Thomas and Margaret Thomas. Special thanks to the series editors, Carol Adams, Paula Bartley and Cathy Loxton, and to Stephanie Boyd and Sally Taylor at Cambridge University Press.

The author and publisher would like to thank the following for permission to reproduce illustrations:

p.19 BBC Hulton Picture Library; p.28 British Library Newspaper Library; pp. 13, 36 The Illustrated London News Picture Library; pp. 4, 9, 10, 11, 14, 16, 20, 21, 22, 23, 24, 25, 26, 31, 33, 34, 35 (*top and bottom*), 37, 44 by courtesy of the Trustees of the Imperial War Museum; pp. 7, 18 (*bottom*), 29, 40 (*left and right*), 41 Mary Evans Picture Library.

Cover illustration: Land Army Girls (*Imperial War Museum*)

Title page: WAACs on parade outside their billet in Rouen, northern France, 1917 (*Imperial War Museum*)

A note on money

Old currency

12*d* (old pennies) = 1*s* (shilling)
20*s* = £1

Modern currency (since 1970)

100p (new pence) = £1

Therefore:

1*d* = about ½p	2*s* = 10p
6*d* = 2½p	5*s* = 25p
1*s* = 5p	10*s* = 50p

Remember that the value of money was very different in the past. To work out the real value you should compare the wages people received with how much they had to pay for food, rent, etc.

Contents

1 Women and the First World War 5

The sources 5
The outbreak of war 5

2 War work 6

The early months of war 6
The need for many hands 6
Women in munitions 10
Women transport workers 12
In the Land Army 14
Nursing and army work 15
When the men returned 17

3 Living through the war 19

Food problems 19
The rent strikes 22
Control of women 23
Motherhood 25
Separation allowances 26
The absence and death of friends
and relatives 28

4 Women at the Front 30

Working at the Front 30
Living at the Front 33
Dangers at the Front 36

5 Fighting for peace 38

The Women's International League
for Permanent Peace 38
The Women's Peace Crusade 40
No Conscription Fellowship 42
Individual acts of resistance 42

6 Conclusion 45

Questions 46

Further reading 47

Glossary 48

Poster to recruit women for the Women's Royal Air Force, which was formed in early 1918. The First World War opened up many new opportunities for British women to work at home and abroad.

1 Women and the First World War

When you think about women and the First World War, what comes to mind? Perhaps you think of women working in *munitions* factories, or as nurses, or of women who never married because their fiancés were killed in the war? Maybe you don't even associate the First World War with women, but think that the war was just a male affair? The First World War was not only about campaigns and battles. It was the first war ever to affect and involve an entire civilian population. Women in Britain participated in the war in many more ways than history books usually suggest, and their lives were greatly changed by it.

The sources

To uncover information about women's lives during the First World War we have to look at many kinds of source material. This book has used newspapers, autobiographies, diaries, letters, interviews with women who lived through the war, official reports, photographs and posters. But it is not easy to find out about all aspects of women's lives during the war. Here are some of the reasons why:

Material written during and after the war tends to focus upon the campaigns and battles, rather than the experiences of ordinary people.

Most of the sources on women, particularly official reports and national newspapers, report on women's war work. Very few include the domestic and personal side of their lives.

Women's experiences and opinions varied according to their social background, age, occupation and domestic situation. Some women's views were expressed in newspapers and journals, particularly those of women's and labour organisations, but they were not necessarily representative of *all* women's opinions.

- Many women's voices were not heard at all.

It is also important to question the reliability of the actual sources available on women in the First World War:

- This book has extensively used interviews with women who lived through the war (oral history). The interviews took place in the 1970s and 1980s. Years after an event we often see it differently. So, although oral history provides a vivid account of the past, it is important to use it alongside other primary sources.

- Oral history, autobiographies, diaries and letters provide one person's personal experience and interpretation of the war. We should read other material and study statistics to discover if one person's experience was unique or representative of others.

- Newspapers, magazines and journals usually hold a political viewpoint. It is therefore important to look at a variety of different approaches and to note issues they ignore as well as those they cover.

- Official reports, reports of political organisations and parliamentary papers are also written from one viewpoint. When reading them, we should try and find out something about the writer or the organisation and the purpose of the report.

The outbreak of war

At 11 pm on 4 August 1914 Britain declared war upon Germany. Now Germany and Austria were at war against Britain, France, Russia and Serbia. Most people in Britain expected a swift and successful end to the war. But before the year was out, it had become obvious that the war was going to be a long one. Indeed, it lasted more than four years and greatly changed the lives of women as well as men.

2 War work

The early months of war

During the First World War the number of women in paid work greatly increased and women started doing many new jobs. But the immediate effect of the war was mass unemployment among both women and men. There were many reasons for this. Trade with Germany stopped, trading routes to other countries were cut off, many middle- and upper-class women dismissed their servants, and some employers simply shut down their factories in the initial war panic. For a short time, in September 1914, as many as 44 per cent of all women workers were unemployed.

Most unemployed men were able to join the forces. But what happened to the women?

Many charitable funds were set up to help the unemployed. The Prince of Wales made an appeal for donations to be made to the National Relief Fund. This became the largest fund of its kind and it was prepared to help anyone who was out of work. Unemployed men and women received 10 shillings a week if they lived in London, and 8 shillings if they lived outside London. Other funds, such as the Women's Golfers Fund, were for certain women only. This fund aimed to find employment for all middle-class women thrown out of work by the war.

Workrooms were also set up. These provided working-class women with employment such as dressmaking, toymaking and cleaning, and paid them 10 shillings a week. However, in practice the women at these workrooms did not always actually work. As Helen Bentwich, a middle-class woman who was involved in running a workroom in West London, described in her autobiography:

> If there isn't enough work for the girls, they have to have lessons – from amateurs, including me – and receive their wages all the same.
>
> *Helen Bentwich, If I Forget Thee: some Chapters of Autobiography 1912–20, 1973*

These lessons were usually on how women should run their homes and look after their children.

The need for many hands

By the summer of 1915 the situation had changed, and there was even a shortage of workers in some areas. There were two main reasons for this – both reasons were to do with the war situation. First, food, clothing and armaments had to be provided for the men fighting in the army and navy. Second, as the war continued, more and more men joined the forces and their jobs had to be filled.

Women were already beginning to replace men in offices and in transport work. But male trade unionists were reluctant to see women take men's places, particularly in industry. They feared that because women were paid less than men, when the men returned from war, they would either get less money, or the women would be kept on instead of them. To avoid this, many of the male trade unions made agreements with either the government or their employers to protect their jobs and wages. Most agreements stated that men could have their jobs back when they returned from the war.

In most jobs women were still paid lower wages than the men they were replacing. Many people argued that it was wrong that a single woman might earn the same as a man supporting a whole family. Others believed that if women did the same work as men, they should be paid the same.

Even the trade union agreements which guaranteed men's jobs did not prevent hostility from some male workers. Whilst many women worked with men on a friendly basis, others remember how the men refused to help them. Elsa Thomas, a working-class woman who did a training course at Woolwich Arsenal, the

'Women's Right to Serve' procession in London, 1915. Both employers and trade unionists were reluctant to see women working in men's jobs, particularly in munitions factories. On 17 July, women marched in this huge procession to show their readiness to offer their services to the war effort. The long banner reads 'The Men of the Empire are Fighting – The Women of the Empire are Working'.

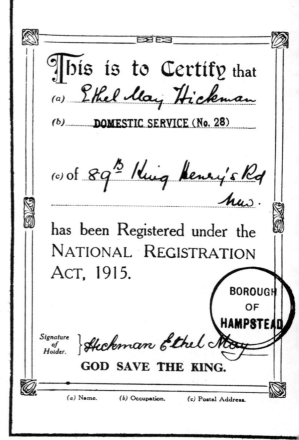

A National Registration Act certificate. In August 1915 all women and men between the ages of 16 and 65 had to register their personal details. This was to let the government know who was available for work. They had to carry the certificate with them at all times.

famous munitions factory in south-east London, recalls:

> They didn't want to show us their livelihood.
> You see, they knew it was their livelihood.
> Women were coming in, you see. They were
> going to cut the wages.
>
> *Elsa Thomas, Interview, Imperial War Museum*

Despite the hostility of some men, women entered nearly all kinds of paid work during the war. Some of these jobs had been considered unsuitable for women before the war. As well as working in munitions and other factories, women became bus and tram conductresses, railway ticket collectors, postwomen and policewomen. They joined the forces and nursing units, they worked on the land, went into offices, they cleaned roads, heaved coal, swept chimneys and worked in gasworks and breweries. These were just some of the paid jobs women did. Many of these women joined trade unions. In 1914, a total of 433,679 women belonged to unions. By 1918 this number had nearly trebled to 1,209,278.

The number of women in paid work during the First World War increased by over a million. Many women left domestic service and went to work elsewhere. Other women left the low-paid, traditionally 'female' trades such as cotton, silk, lace, tailoring, millinery and pottery. But where did the extra 1.4 million women come from? Many married, widowed and retired women who had left paid work went back into the workforce; school leavers

Number of women in paid work in 1914 and 1918

	July 1914	July 1918	increase (%)
Self-employed and employers	430,000	470,000	9
Industry	2,178,600	2,970,600	36
Domestic service	1,658,000	1,258,000	− 24
Commerce	505,500	934,500	85
National and local government (including teaching)	262,200	460,200	76
Agriculture	190,000	228,000	20
Hotels, public houses and theatre	181,000	220,000	22
Transport	18,200	117,200	544
Others ie professional, home-workers, etc.	542,500	652,000	20
Total employed	5,966,000	7,310,500	23

Based on the Report from the War Cabinet Committee on Women in Industry, 1919

Working in a bacteriological laboratory in Glasgow. Many women took on skilled work for the first time during the war.

immediately got jobs; and a few middle- and upper-class women who had not previously worked also took up paid employment.

Women in munitions

About 900,000 women were involved in making shells, guns and aircraft for the British forces. Many of these women worked in large munitions factories, and most were working-class. They did a wide range of jobs, such as making bullets and shells, assembling detonators, polishing the time fuses and shells, and filling the shells with gunpowder. One woman worker described in an interview how she used to fill the shells, before machines were introduced to help with the job:

> We had to stem the powder into shells with broom handles and mallets. You see, you'd have your shell . . . and the broom handle and your tin of powder. And you'd put a bit in, stem it down, put a bit more in, stem it down. It took all your time to get it all in; it was very hard work.
>
> *Elsie McIntyre, Interview, Imperial War Museum*

Elsie McIntyre had to be careful at work, as she filled the shells with a poisonous substance known as TNT (trinitrotoluene), which was used to make explosives. Although women did wear protective clothing, such as respirators and veils, long exposure to TNT turned their skin and hair yellow. They were then nicknamed 'canaries'. Some women died in explosions at work and there were many minor accidents. At least 300 munitions women were either killed as a result of explosions or died from TNT poisoning, but the exact number will never be known.

Women munition workers saw many changes in factory life during the war. For

Women working in a munitions factory at Chilwell in Nottingham. The shells have been filled with gunpowder.

10

The unbeaten football team of the 'Palmers Munitionettes'. Large workplaces organised activities such as football and basketball for their women workers. Notice their sporting outfits — shorts were most 'daring' for the time. The works' nurse always accompanied the team to matches.

example, women began to wear trousers, as they were easier to work in than long skirts. In some factories new canteens were built; in others, rest rooms, ambulance rooms and first aid appliances were provided. And, as many women with children worked in munitions, some factories introduced temporary crèche facilities.

The most important change in factory life was the introduction of the Lady Welfare Supervisor. The Lady Welfare Supervisor was a middle- or upper-class woman with a wide range of duties. These included hiring female labour, dealing with workers' housing problems, keeping order and discipline at work, and telling women workers how to dress and behave. The government believed that the introduction of Lady Welfare Supervisors was very successful: welfare supervision had,

> . . . tended towards creating a better class of 'factory girl'.
>
> *Ministry of Labour papers, November 1917*

By the end of the war, there were more than 1,000 Lady Welfare Supervisors operating in munitions factories.

However, the Supervisors had a considerable amount of control over the lives of the female workers, and were not always popular. This extract describing the Lady Welfare Supervisor is taken from an article written by a woman worker:

> Here is a person introduced to 'get more out of us' and whether this is done by running clubs

and organising dances, or by the older cruder methods, this person remains suspect as the paid official in the service of the employer.

Women's Trade Union Review, April 1917

Why did so many women work in munitions? They were closely supervised, their work was often dangerous and they also worked very long hours. At the beginning of the war they worked as long as 12 hours a day, plus overtime, with sometimes only one day off a month. (Later on, the hours were reduced in some factories, as it was found that such long hours were counter-productive.)

Below, three women give their different reasons for going into munitions factories. Amy May had been in domestic service before the war. She went to work in the Woolwich Arsenal in London:

That was where they wanted people most . . . that's where they kept saying, you know, your King and country needs you.

Amy May, Interview, Imperial War Museum

Elsie Farlow left her job in a cotton mill and went to the Royal Ordinance Works in Coventry:

I wanted to be as big as any of the other girls, you know, who'd left the weaving, and go on munitions.

Elsie Farlow, Interview, Imperial War Museum

Isabella Clarke went from Ireland to work in a munitions factory in Morecambe:

. . . for the money, because there wasn't much of a chance in Belfast to get a decent job.

Isabella Clarke, Interview, Imperial War Museum

Munitions work was certainly one of the best paid jobs for women during the war. Although some munition workers were only paid between £1 and 30 shillings a week, some women earned as much as £5 a week. When we compare this sum with the average weekly wage of 11s 7d paid to women industrial workers before the war, munitions work must have seemed very attractive.

Women transport workers

The area where there was the most dramatic increase in women workers during the war was in transport (see table p.9). Before the war 18,200 women worked in transport. Most of these were railway cleaners, attendants and clerks. By 1918, 117,200 women worked in transport as bus and tram conductresses, railway ticket collectors, signal women, porters and district examiners. The table on page 13 shows the jobs where women replaced men on the railways.

Women transport workers faced opposition from both the men they were working with and the men they were replacing. Trade unions made agreements with their employers to protect men's jobs for when they returned from war. At work some women faced harassment from male colleagues. A conductress on the trams in Southampton, for example, remembered how one driver would deliberately drive very fast:

The tram used to sway an' he'd turn round to me and he'd give me such a grin. He knew I wasn't used to that.

Annie Fry, Interview, Southampton Museum

At least Annie Fry was paid the same as male tram conductors. In most other areas of paid work, women had to accept lower wages than men. When women were accepted as workers on the tramways and the bus services however, the principle of 'equal pay for equal work' was agreed upon. This meant that if women did the same work as the men they were paid the same. But in August 1918 a *war bonus* of 5 shillings a week was granted to the men only. Women bus and tram conductresses in London went on strike to demand this bonus. The strike soon spread to many other places including Bath, Brighton and Weston-super-Mare. Some male trade unionists refused to support the women. They claimed that many of the women were servicemen's wives and did not need the money. Others supported the strike, but as we can see from this newspaper report, it was not always the

Number of women employed by the railways

	July 1914	July 1918
Booking clerks	152	3,612
Telegraph and telephone operators and other clerks	2,800	20,995
Ticket collectors	—	1,972
Carriage cleaners	214	4,603
Engine cleaners	—	3,065
Porters and checkers	3	9,980
Workshop labourers	43	2,547
Other labourers	420	580
Cooks, waitresses, attendants on stations and trains	1,239	3,642
Signal and points women, gatekeepers, guards and conductors	437	1,292
Munitions, machinists and gaugers	44	1,082
Painters and cleaners	698	1,177
Total (including occupations not separately specified)	12,423	65,887

A.W. Kirkaldy, British Labour, Replacement and Conciliation, 1914–21, 1921

women's interests they had in mind. Robert Williams of the Transport Workers' Federation feared that if women were paid less:

> This will be detrimental to the men on *demobilisation*, and if the principle is not settled now, it will lead to a sex war when this war is over, which will be deplorable.
>
> *The Herald [a Labour newspaper], 21 August 1918*

The women eventually won the strike, but first they brought London and other towns to a virtual halt.

As in munitions, most of the women who worked as bus and tram conductresses and for the railways were working-class. Usually middle- and upper-class women were only employed as supervisors and inspectors. Let us now look at work that was done mainly by middle- and upper-class women.

A couple of newly recruited railway porters at Marylebone Station in London, 1915. Later on women porters were given uniforms to wear.

In the Land Army

In 1914 there were about 100,000 women working full-time on the land, and nearly as many again working on a casual basis. But despite the large numbers of women who did work on the land, many areas of agricultural work were considered the male preserve, and unsuitable for women. Many people thought that women were not physically strong enough to perform heavy manual labour. Some people also argued that women should not be involved in dirty work.

During the war, however, Britain needed to grow more of its own food. At the same time many men were *enlisting*. So more women were asked to help on the land.

Yet local women were difficult to find. Many local women went to work in factories where wages were usually higher than the

Women of the Forestry Corps felling a tree.

8–20 shillings a week paid to agricultural workers. Sometimes women found that their husbands did not want them to work on the land. This attitude is shown in an inquiry carried out in Lincoln in 1919:

Some of the labourers on the Wold who were not used to their wives going out said that the same standard of comfort and cleanliness was impossible in their homes under the new conditions.

Wages and Conditions of Employment in Agriculture, 1919

What could be done to solve this shortage of labour? Various voluntary organisations sent out members to work on the land, but they still did not provide enough women. So early in 1917 the Women's Land Army was formed under the direction of the government. Most of the women who joined the Land Army were middle- and upper-class. Some were able to work part-time near their homes. Others, particularly single women, were sent away to farms where they usually worked 10–12 hours a day, 6 days a week. By 1918, the number of women working on the land full-time had increased to 113,000.

Women could join one of three sections of the Land Army – agriculture, timber-cutting and forage (looking after foodstuffs for animals). Women in the agricultural section did many different kinds of work. These included tending sheep, picking potatoes, hoeing, ploughing, helping with the harvest and working on market gardens. An account of agricultural life written by a woman from Bristol shows how many different jobs one woman might do:

I was 17 yrs and was bored . . . I decided to join the Land Army. My first start was to Bishops Lydeard [Somerset] for 3 months training, general farm work, milking etc. Having finished, my next trip was to a small farm near Wineaton . . . From there I was posted to Lincolnshire for the back-aching job of picking up potatoes . . . Whilst there the war was declared over . . . [I] moved on to Kent threshing . . . The men still having not returned I was sent back to a farm at Cuckington [Somerset] where we did general work, also butter and cheese making.

Mrs Price, private letter, March 1984

Women in the Land Army either slept in a room in the farmhouse, in a farm labourer's cottage, or on the floor of a spare barn. They usually paid 15 shillings a week for their food and lodging.

Discipline was strict in the Land Army. Once women had signed up for either six months or a year, they could not leave without special permission. If they broke their agreement they had to pay a £2 fine. Women were also punished for minor offences, particularly in the forage section:

Grace Smith of the Women's Army Forage Department was at Gloucester yesterday sentenced to 14 days' hard labour for being absent from work without leave.

Newspaper cutting from the Arncliffe Sennett Collection

This was, however, an exceptional case. Most of the women who joined the Land Army seem to have been happy. They would probably agree with Mrs Price when she said, 'But with it all we really enjoyed ourselves'.

Nursing and army work

Many middle- and upper-class women also became nurses, worked directly for the army, or joined one of the women's services. Some of these women had a chance to work abroad (see Chapter 4). Others worked in military hospitals and army bases in Britain.

Life was not easy for such women. Few had worked before the war. Now they were working very long day and night shifts. As Angela, Countess of Limerick, said, 'We never stopped for one single instant'. The Countess worked as a *Voluntary Aid Detachment (VAD)* nurse at a hospital in Surrey. The Voluntary Aid Detachment was an organisation set up to provide help for the sick and wounded, in case of an enemy invasion. Below, the Countess describes her work:

You'd come on duty at 8, and you'd have to do all the temperatures and dressings to start off with. Then you'd have to clean all the instruments afterwards and the trolleys and get them all ready for the next lot of dressings . . . Then you'd have again four-hourly dressings and temperatures and things like that and then there'd be the men's dinners . . . Well then in the afternoon there would be special duties. I mean some days you'd have to clean the lockers and other days you'd have to polish the floor . . . and then again we had the men's teas and then in the evenings there'd be all the dressings and temperatures and washing and that sort of thing to do before the night staff came on at 8.

Countess of Limerick, Interview, Imperial War Museum

For this work the VADs were at first unpaid, and from 1915 they were paid £20 a year. Although they had free board and lodgings, they had to buy their uniform out of their earnings.

Some VAD nurses faced hostility from the trained and established nurses. They resented these inexperienced VAD nurses who entered the hospitals and learned nursing 'on the job'. In the army, women faced hostility too, but this time from the men.

Poster to recruit women with the Voluntary Aid Detachment. VADs performed a wide range of jobs: possible destinations for recruits are listed.

One woman, for example, Elizabeth Lee, became a driver in the Army Service Corps. She was put on a month's trial period and decided despite constant harassment to stay. The men resented the women because every time a woman went into an army base in Britain, a man was usually sent overseas to the fighting line:

> They [the men] led us a devil of a life . . . They cut a petrol pipe half through, they'd unscrew a valve on there, they'd change over the leads on the . . . sparking plugs . . . They'd empty oil out of your lamps . . . they would give us the wrong directions.
>
> *Elizabeth Lee, Interview, Imperial War Museum*

Elizabeth's first job was delivering food, laundry and letters to the petrol posts along the south coast of England. If someone was ill she had to go out in the ambulance. Her working hours were very long – sometimes from 7am to 10pm. It could be dangerous work:

> We were never allowed any lights on our vehicles when we were driving along the coast out there after dark. There were no signposts; you had to know your way.
>
> *Elizabeth Lee, Interview, Imperial War Museum*

Despite the long hours, both Elizabeth Lee and the Countess of Limerick enjoyed their work. If it had not been for the war they would never have had the chance to do it. This was the same for many women. But what happened when the war ended and the men came home?

When the men returned

Women were no longer wanted in their war-time jobs. They were demobilised from the army and nursing units; and as the men returned they wanted their jobs back in factories, on the land, in transport and in offices. Many of these jobs were protected for the men by trade union agreements. For those jobs which were not protected the government passed a special Act of Parliament in August 1919. It was called the Restoration of Pre-War Practices Act. Clauses 1 and 2 of the Act, summarised here, meant that most women had to leave their jobs:

> Any rule, practice or custom departed from during the war are to be restored.
>
> Where new branches have been established within an industry, pre-war practices are to apply to it.

Women were expected to go back to the home or to return to the traditionally 'female' trades and domestic service.

Some women, particularly single women, were reluctant to leave their new jobs. These women were strongly criticised by the popular press and the unions. But many women with children were only too ready to leave their jobs. The conditions of war work had only added to their double burden of doing paid work and domestic work. These women had often worked twelve-hour shifts throughout the war, with perhaps an hour's journey to and from work. When they reached home they not only had children to feed and the cleaning and cooking to do, but they also had to queue for food. As early as the autumn of 1916 letters were appearing in the journal *Labour Woman* saying that:

> [Women] will be glad to leave off their present men's work. I notice that they often seem to feel the work a heavy strain, and in munitions factories I believe a good many married women would be only too glad to stop now . . .
>
> *Labour Woman [the monthly journal of the Women's Labour League], 1916*

By 1921 most women had left their war-time jobs. Yet, the valuable experience of their war work could not be taken away from them. Women had proved that they were capable of doing work which before the war had only been done by men. Many single women had moved away from home for the first time. Women had earned higher wages than before the war; and for many women the friendships they made at work lasted for many years. The war had allowed women to stand on their own feet. And as one woman, who was no longer financially dependent on her husband, said:

> I'd never known what it was to be a free woman before.
>
> *C. S. Peel, How We Lived Then 1914–18, 1929*

National Projectile Factory, **Templeborough, Sheffield.**

An Appreciation of loyal services rendered by *Frances Peart. 2741.* during the Great War, 1914-1918, as *Gauger* from *May 1916* to *December 1918* at the NATIONAL PROJECTILE FACTORY, where 2,500,000 SHELLS were turned out to Feed the Guns.

Thos. Firth & Sons, Ltd.,

Oliver Sander.

General Manager.

Christmas, 1918.

Edward Kay

Sophia K. Davies

Certificate of appreciation given to a munition worker at the end of the war.

War work was only part of the story, though. Not only did the First World War provide many new job opportunities for women, but it also had a great effect on everyday life.

Women over the age of 30, voting for the first time in the 1918 general election. Although many women had fought for the right to vote since the turn of the century, women did not win the vote until after the war. Some people believe that they finally won the vote because of their important contribution to the war effort.

Food problems

The price of food doubled during the war. Many basic foodstuffs, such as margarine, meat, potatoes, sugar and tea, became scarce. There were a number of reasons for this. Some people bought more food than they needed: they hoarded food. The bad harvest of 1916 caused further shortages. And German boats sank many British ships carrying food, hoping to starve Britain into surrendering.

As a result, mealtimes became a worry for women. Men were not so aware of the problems women faced, as few shopped or cooked. These jobs were seen as a woman's responsibility. So how did the women cope?

Some women bought cheap hot meals from new cost-price restaurants and national kitchens. At the end of 1914, the *Women's Freedom League* set up one of the first cost-price restaurants in Nine Elms, London. This restaurant sold 250 meals a day. On 21 May 1917, the Ministry of Food, a new government department, set up the first national kitchen. Women could buy meals from this national kitchen and take them home to eat. Within a year there were 535 of these kitchens. Both the national kitchens and the cost-price restaurants cooked food in large quantities, and did not sell meals to make a profit. It was therefore cheaper for women to buy meals from them,

Protesting against the price of milk, 1916: one of many demonstrations against food prices and shortages.

than to buy the food and cook it themselves. It also saved a lot of time, as this report on the national kitchens points out:

> A woman who is working all day outside her home has no time to cook and the children suffer. Where there are public kitchens it is found that mothers give the children pence with which to buy hot, nourishing food, and often they buy food which only needs reheating for their own suppers.
>
> *Women's War Work Collection, Imperial War Museum*

As the food shortages became worse, queues were often seen outside shops. Working-class women, and middle-class women who had no servants to queue for them, spent hours waiting to buy food and coal. Often women who were working would send their children to buy food. This letter in a newspaper gives us some idea of how frustrating this could be:

> My daughter went out at 7 am to the Maypole Dairy Co. shop and after waiting till 10.30 am was turned away without any margarine, came home chilled to the bone besides losing her education. If we could have a system of rationing, I believe these hardships could be overcome.
>
> *Workers' Dreadnought [a weekly newspaper of the East London Federation of Suffragettes, and edited by Sylvia Pankhurst], 19 January 1918*

But it was only a few months before the end of the war – on 25 February 1918 – that the government finally introduced *rationing*.

Ration card: cards like this were introduced in February 1918, and were initially used for butter and margarine. Notice the space for the rationing of other items later on.

…vernment poster, 1917. British ships carrying food were under constant attack from German U-boats. …opaganda urged women to cater carefully as food was in short supply.

Food queue: a common sight during the war. If women were working they would often send their children to queue for the family's food.

The rent strikes

Women also faced difficulties posed by rising rents. Early in the war many people began to refuse paying their rent. Why did they do this?

The munitions factories and shipyards in major cities needed more workers. The local population were already working in these factories and shipyards, and many more people arrived from smaller towns and the countryside to join the workforces. With large numbers of extra people in the cities it became very difficult to find somewhere to live. Then the landlords began to put up the rents, believing that the tenants would take in lodgers to pay for these increases. But they were wrong. The tenants refused to pay the increases and went on rent strike. Some women in Glasgow led the most effective and well-known of these strikes.

In late 1914 and early 1915 the women of Clydeside, Glasgow, met in their kitchens, in the streets, and in huge outside demonstrations. They demanded that the government should stop landlords from increasing their rents. They called landlords 'the enemy at home'. When landlords raised the rents yet again in May 1915, the women refused to pay the increase, and a struggle followed between the tenants and landlords. The landlords got permission from the law courts to throw tenants out of their houses. But when the court officer arrived to evict the tenants, the women stopped him from doing so. Helen Crawfurd, a local middle-class woman who helped to organise the rent strike, tells us how the women did this:

Air-raid damage in London. Air raids were yet another problem women at home had to face. During the war some coastal towns were attacked by enemy warships and cities bombed from the air. The total number of civilian casualties from Zeppelin and aeroplane raids was 1,570.

One woman with a bell would sit in the close, or passage, watching while the other women in the tenement went on with their household duties. Whenever the Bailiff's officer appeared to evict a tenant the woman in the passage immediately rang the bell, and the women came from all parts of the building, some with flour, if baking, wet clothes, if washing and other missiles. Usually the Bailiff made off for his life, chased by a mob of angry women.

Helen Crawfurd, unpublished autobiography

By October 1915 about 15,000 tenants in Glasgow were on rent strike. The government still refused to do anything to help and the women became more determined than ever. More than 4,000 women marched to the city hall in Glasgow. This newspaper report shows what the women planned to do if the rent increases were not stopped:

'We lodge the munitions workers' said one housewife, 'and we shall keep them in bed for a day or two if we do not get our rents reduced'. Another mother said that she would tell her son to come home [from the trenches].

Woman Worker [the monthly journal of the National Federation of Women Workers], January 1916

Even more tenants refused to pay their rents, and on 17 November 1915, eighteen munition workers on rent strike were put on trial. The Women's Housing Association urged the shipyard and munition workers to stop work for a day and to march with them to the court to demand that the government act. About 10,000 people demonstrated outside the court. The court dropped the case and the government soon introduced the first ever Rent Restriction Act. Rents everywhere in Britain were to stay at their pre-war level. The women had won their demands.

Control of women

Before 1914 the social lives of young single women were carefully controlled. Upper- and middle-class girls were usually accompanied by *chaperones* whenever they went out or had visitors at home. Young working-class women were also restricted. Although they did not have chaperones, they were not allowed to stay out late, and were expected home in good time to help with jobs around the house.

During the First World War, however, young women of all classes enjoyed much greater social freedom.

As many single women moved away from home for the first time during the war, their parents could no longer supervise their leisure. Some women also had more money than before the war and were now financially independent. So they began going out on their own to dances, to restaurants, to the theatre and to cinemas. A few women began to smoke in public. Many women found that long hair and long skirts were impractical for the kind of work they were now doing, so they cut their hair and wore shorter skirts or trousers.

Some people were not happy about this greater freedom for women. They particularly disliked women going into public houses. Whilst it remained socially unacceptable for upper- and middle-class women to go into pubs, some working-class women did frequent them. On Saturday nights police constables, bishops and magistrates stood outside pubs and counted the number of women going in. Some wrote to newspapers complaining that women were spending all their time getting drunk:

> The Bishop of Liverpool said the other day . . . that drink was now most deadly amongst women. He could speak of a street in which almost every woman was drinking and demoralised. The Bishop of London . . . also said quite recently that the East End clergy told him that they had never known such an orgy of drinking among women as during the last 12 months.
>
> *White Ribbon [the monthly newspaper of the British Women's Temperance Association], December 1915*

Special Patrols of the Women's Police Service, which was formed during the war. Their activities included supervising music halls and cinemas, patrolling railway stations and parks, and attending police courts.

However, if we look at official reports on the number of women convicted of drunkenness, we find that it actually decreased by a huge amount during the war. In 1914, 37,311 women were charged with being drunk. In 1918 only 7,222 women were convicted of drunkenness. When asked in an interview (Imperial War Museum) if she went into pubs, Elsie Farlow, a munitions worker in Coventry, said 'Oo no, you never went in pubs in those days'. The evidence seems to suggest that only some women went into pubs and very few of them actually got drunk.

Similar charges of drunkenness were made against men workers and soldiers, so the government introduced licensing laws for women and men. But in some towns it was only the women who were stopped from drinking. For example, in Plymouth, pubs did not sell women drinks after 6pm, whereas men could buy drinks until 9pm. In London, women, unlike men, could not buy a drink before 11.30am. In Hartlepool, pubs stopped selling drinks to women altogether. When women protested at this ruling, Mr Bladon of the Police Court Mission in Hartlepool said:

> [The ruling] was for the protection of women, just as a parent might put a guard round the fire to protect the children.
>
> *The Vote [the weekly newspaper of the Women's Freedom League], 12 October 1917*

Buying a drink in a pub was not the only example of new rules being introduced, which treated women differently from men. Rules were also passed during the war to control women's sexual behaviour, but not men's.

The spread of sexually transmitted diseases, especially *venereal disease* (VD), amongst men in the army and navy, alarmed many people. They feared it would affect men's ability to fight in the war. But instead of regulating men's sexual behaviour, the government and the military turned to women. For example, in 1914, the Commanding Officer in Cardiff ordered all women 'of a certain class' to stay at home between 7pm and 8am. Exactly who was of this 'class' of women was up to the Commanding Officer. This meant that any woman could be arrested for being out at ight. Soon five women were arrested and imprisoned for being out after 7pm. Many women were very angry about this, and wrote to the police, to the War Office and to newspapers:

> This order [is] highly dangerous to respectable women who are liable to be charged with an offence unknown to the ordinary law and tried in an irregular way before an arbitrary court without adequate opportunity to defend themselves.
>
> *Women's Dreadnought, 5 December 1914*

s a result of these protests, the Commanding Officer released the women and withdrew the order.

Similar instances happened throughout the war. Then in March 1918 the government passed a new order, called Regulation 40D. It said that if a woman with VD had sexual intercourse with a man in the army or navy, or even asked him to, she would be imprisoned. If a man with VD infected a woman, on the other hand, he would not be prosecuted. Also, if any soldier or sailor claimed that a woman had given him VD, she was to be medically examined. In some cases his led to men making false accusations. Many women were outraged by the regulation. One woman wrote:

> The regulation of course does not make it in any way a crime for a man to infect a woman, but only for a woman to infect a man and his bare word is apparently taken as sufficient proof that there has been communication with one another . . . It appears very likely that men are bringing such charges from pure malice, for it must be noted that something like 50 % of the prosecutions fail because the woman proves under examination that she is innocent.
>
> *Labour Woman, September 1918*

The government held a different view on the matter and claimed that most prosecutions of men succeeded. At a War Office conference July 1918, it was stated that:

> The regulation has only been in force a limited time, but already there have been a great number of prosecutions under it, and a good many convictions.
>
> *War Office papers, July 1918*

Advertisement for a Ball in Middlewich, Cheshire, in 1919. Money raised by this Ball was to go towards special Cards of Thanks for the men of the town who had fought in the Forces.

The War Office did admit that the regulation was one-sided but it remained in force until the end of the war.

Motherhood

Towards the end of the war, newspapers and magazines began telling women that the greatest work for them was the care of children:

> It seems fitting that women's attention should be turned to the importance of the baby at this juncture. After all there is no finer work in which women can engage, no higher duty for them to perform, no way in which they can better serve the Empire than by caring for the young.
>
> *Lady's Pictorial [a magazine for middle- and upper-class women], 7 July 1917*

And in 1916 Mother's Day was introduced. This emphasised again the importance of motherhood.

Many people also became more accepting of women who gave birth to illegitimate children, particularly when the father of the child was a soldier or sailor. Many lives were being lost in the war and the care of every child became important. As the newly formed National Council for the Unmarried Mother and her Child stressed in a leaflet on its aims:

> The drain on the manhood of the nation makes life-saving action all the more imperative.
> *Women's War Work Collection, Imperial War Museum*

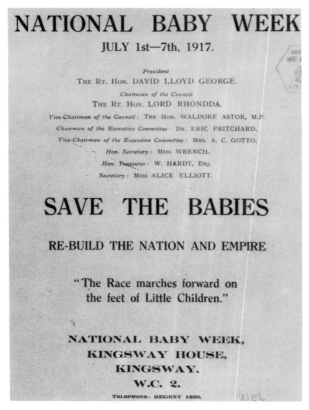

NATIONAL BABY WEEK

JULY 1st—7th, 1917.

President
The Rt. Hon. DAVID LLOYD GEORGE.

Chairman of the Council
The Rt. Hon. LORD RHONDDA.

Vice-Chairman of the Council: The Hon. WALDORF ASTOR, M.P.

Chairman of the Executive Committee: Dr. ERIC PRITCHARD.

Vice-Chairman of the Executive Committee: Mrs. A. C. GOTTO.

Hon. Secretary: Miss WRENCH.

Hon. Treasurer: W. HARDY, Esq.

Secretary: Miss ALICE ELLIOTT.

SAVE THE BABIES

RE-BUILD THE NATION AND EMPIRE

"The Race marches forward on the feet of Little Children."

NATIONAL BABY WEEK, KINGSWAY HOUSE, KINGSWAY, W.C. 2.

TELEPHONE: REGENT 1890.

Poster advertising the National Baby Week in July 1917, which drew public attention to the importance of protecting babies' lives. Another National Baby Week was held the following year.

Amidst this concern for the future of the race, women won a great victory. For years the *Women's Co-operative Guild* had been campaigning for better maternity conditions. In 1918 the government passed the Maternity and Child Welfare Act. This provided many new services, including free hospital treatment for children under the age of five; and food allowances for expectant and nursing mothers and for children under five.

Separation allowances

What happened to the families of men who went away to fight in the war? How did they make ends meet? The government paid a weekly sum of money to all wives of soldiers and sailors. It also paid a sum to any other relative who had been financially dependent on a serviceman before he enlisted. This sum of money was called a separation allowance. By 1917 the government was paying more than three million women a separation allowance. If the man was killed in the war the separation allowance then became a pension.

The amount women received depended on the rank of the serviceman, whether he was in the army or navy, and how many children there were. The amount paid also increased during the war. For example, a woman married to a soldier at the lowest rank received 12s 6d a week throughout most of the war. Wives of sailors at the lowest rank received 11 shillings.

Often women had to wait five or six weeks before they received their separation allowance. This meant much suffering for the poorer women:

> Mrs G. – 2 children with measles and 1 with pneumonia, no food in house and no money since August 15th. Reservist's wife.
> *Women's Dreadnought, 5 September 1914*

To cope with these difficulties women formed their own organisations. The largest one, the League of Rights for Soldiers' and Sailors' Wives and Female Relatives, was set up in the East End of London in February 1915. Its aims were:

Letter sent to Minnie Farrington's mother (see page 29) following the death of her husband. Her separation allowance was to continue for 26 weeks: after that she received a pension.

To protect the interests of all wives, mothers and other relatives of soldiers and sailors; to secure for them adequate Separation Allowances and Pensions; to act on their behalf in all cases of neglect and delay, and generally to obtain an improvement in their conditions.

Leaflet on the Aims of the League of Rights for Soldiers' and Sailors' Wives and Relatives, War Emergency Workers National Committee material, Labour Party Archives

Once women were regularly receiving their separation allowance they met other problems. Bishops, magistrates and organisations such as the Catholic Women's League accused soldiers' and sailors' wives of spending their allowance on drink, and neglecting their children. This statement taken from a pamphlet published by a magistrate is an example of what was being said:

In many cases the money being paid to soldiers' and sailors' dependants is 'being shockingly and shamefully wasted'. Many families go dinnerless on Mondays because the women who have drawn the Government money remain in the public house from 11 am till late in the afternoon.

Theophilus Simpson, The Underworld of Manchester in Wartime, 1915

Both soldiers' and sailors' wives, and the National Society for the Prevention of Cruelty to Children (NSPCC) aimed to show that these claims were not true. One hundred and forty-eight branches of the NSPCC inquired into the claims. They found that women had not been spending their separation allowances on drink. Instead:

[Most women have] bought new clothes for their children, paid off back rents and debts and in some cases have opened an account in the Post Office Savings Bank.

The Vote, 22 January 1915

But the government decided to act upon the rumours of drunkenness. It asked the police, schools and charities to keep an eye on servicemen's wives. If the police found these women drunk more than once, they would lose their separation allowance.

Some middle- and upper-class women also listened to the claims, and set up clubs for the working-class wives of soldiers and sailors. These clubs were to encourage women not to go to the pub. At the clubs women could read, write letters or sew. The organisers also gave lectures in subjects like cooking, childcare and hygiene. This was similar to the workrooms (see page 6). Many middle- and upper-class women believed that working-class women did not know how to run their homes properly. This is illustrated in a report on the clubs:

[The lectures were] to educate them in household or other practical ways, so that their homes and children may not be neglected in the absence of their menkind, and to encourage them to save their money, instead of spending it on drink or in other unnecessary directions.

Report of the Women's United Service League, 1915, Women's War Work Collection

THE CRIME OF BEING A SOLDIER'S WIFE.

MAGISTRATE: Do you confess that your husband is serving his country at the Front?
SOLDIER'S WIFE: Yes, Sir,
MAGISTRATE: Then you must be put under police surveillance at once.

Cartoon from the Common Cause, 11 December 1914.

It is not surprising that a lot of women did not like the lectures and did not always go to them. The organiser of a club in Aberdare wrote, 'I fear the lectures have not been so many'. But many women did go to the clubs to meet each other. They could talk about their anxieties over relatives away at war, and share their grief if a loved one had been killed in the war.

The absence and death of friends and relatives

More than six million men went away to war. This was 28 per cent of the male population. An enormous number of these men were wounded (1,676,037); some of them were disabled for life. Many other men were killed in the war (722,785). Nearly all women knew someone who fought in the war and was maimed or killed. How did they cope with this emotional burden?

As soon as a close friend or relative enlisted in the army or navy, life became difficult. Vera Brittain was a middle-class woman from Buxton, and her fiancé was in the army. She recorded her feelings when he left for the Front:

> On every side there seemed to be despair and no way out . . . Every thought brought nothing but darkness and pain.
>
> *Alan Bishop (ed.), Chronicle of Youth: Vera Brittain's War Diary 1915–17, 1980*

She did not hear from her fiancé, Roland, for some weeks. 'It is this anxiety and suspense that wears me out', she wrote. Once his letters started arriving, 'Every ring at the door startles me lest it may be a telegram' bringing bad news.

Life was equally difficult for a Yorkshire woman called Miriam. At the outbreak of the war her son Victor volunteered to go overseas. When he left England on 12 April 1915, Miriam wrote in her diary:

> I cannot restrain myself any longer. I feel overwhelmed with grief.

On the following day she recorded:

> I got through my work somehow, but every moment of every waking hour I am thinking of

TO THE YOUNG WOMEN OF LONDON

Is your "Best Boy" wearing Khaki? If not don't **YOU THINK** he should be?

If he does not think that you and your country are worth fighting for—do you think he is **WORTHY** of you?

Don't pity the girl who is alone—her young man is probably a soldier—fighting for her and her country—and for **YOU.**

If your young man neglects his duty to his King and Country, the time may come when he will **NEGLECT YOU.**

Think it over—then ask him to

JOIN THE ARMY TO-DAY

leaflet showing the pressure put on women to encourage [m]en to enlist. The origin and date of this leaflet is [u]nknown.

him. Indeed, in my opinion, the mothers suffer the most, all the time the suspense is so cruel.

M. Murphy, A Home Fire Burning

However, Miriam was lucky. Her son [r]eturned from the war with only a minor [in]jury. Vera's fiancé, Roland, was killed. A [m]onth after his death Vera confided in her [di]ary:

I wonder if ever, ever I shall get over this feeling of blank hopelessness, of feeling it is cruel that I should have to suffer so, of wishing I had never been born at all.

Alan Bishop (ed.), Chronicle of Youth: Vera Brittain's War Diary 1915–17, 1980

Some women kept going by working all hours of the day and night. Others went to *séances*, hoping to be told of a future reunion with a loved one. And other women carried on for the sake of their children. Minnie Farrington, from Huddersfield, for example, lost her father in the Battle of the Somme in September 1916. Her mother was in a state of shock for a long time. It was only when an aunt offered to take one of the children to live with her that the mother seemed to come back to life. Minnie remembers how:

My mother was like a lioness with her cubs. She said to the aunt, 'These are Roger's children left in my care and we'll face things together'.

Mrs M. Farrington, private letter, April 1984

The emotional burden of war continued long after 1918. Loved ones who had been killed were not forgotten, and many women found themselves caring for a husband or other male relative who returned from the war permanently disabled. Hannah Burchell, a woman from West Sussex, shows how difficult this could be. Her husband was seriously wounded during the war and was unable to work. Hannah had to go to work instead, and also care for her husband. As Hannah recalled:

I had a very tough job because he wasn't well enough. He was so often in and out of hospital. He had 19 operations and he was in a wheelchair for 12 years and I had to lift my husband in and out of bed. Dr. Pepper said to me 'don't'. Dr. Pepper came this morning he said to me 'Mrs Burchell' he said, 'you've ruined yourself. You've worked yourself to a standstill'.

Hannah Burchell, Interview, West Sussex Record Office

We think of the men who died during or as a result of the war each year on 11 November – Remembrance Day. Yet we have forgotten about the women who grieved over the dead and cared for those who were permanently disabled. We have also forgotten about the women who died whilst working at the Front.

4 Women at the Front

It was not only men who went to the Front in the First World War. Women also worked at the Front in hospitals, army bases, canteens and recreation clubs. Although many women went to the war zone, most of the women at the Front lived and worked behind the actual fighting line.

At first the British government did not want women to work at the Front. War was seen as an entirely male activity. So when Mrs McDougall, the organising officer of the *First Aid Nursing Yeomanry (FANY)*, offered the services of her organisation as ambulance drivers in France, the government rejected her offer. The government said that:

It was not considered practical to employ women to drive for the British wounded in France.

Report of the work and organisation of the FANY to 1 November 1917, Imperial War Museum

And when another woman, Dr Elsie Inglis, suggested to the War Office that VADs should be used in army hospitals, she was told to 'go home and keep quiet'.

But Dr Inglis did not go home and keep quiet. Together with other women, she offered her medical services to the Belgian, French and Serbian authorities. This time they were accepted. It was only at a later stage of the war when more men were needed to fight, that the British government reluctantly began to employ women, other than nurses, at the Front.

Working at the Front

Throughout the war, more than 25,000 women went to work at the Front. Few women had had the chance to go abroad before the war. Now women were working in three continents – Europe, Asia and Africa – where they did many different jobs. As well as nursing the wounded, women drove ambulances, ran soup kitchens, put on shows and plays for the soldiers, and worked as cooks, clerks and telephonists in army bases. What were some of these jobs like?

Some women who could drive and knew how to perform first aid became ambulance drivers. They usually drove the wounded either from casualty clearing centres or from ambulance trains to hospital, and then from the hospitals to ships to take them home. A woman ambulance driver, Beryl Hutchinson, who worked for the FANY, remembers how they used to meet the wounded from the ambulance train:

The train came from the Front into Calais station and then they were all taken into a huge big hangar, and then the doctors came round with the list of how many vacant beds there were and they labelled the men with the hospital to which they had to go and then we drivers had to go in and find our own labels . . . For a long time we had to carry our own men out to the ambulance.

Beryl Hutchinson, Interview, Imperial War Museum

The ambulances could carry six men. When carrying the badly wounded Beryl had to drive very slowly and carefully. Another driver, who went to France as a VAD and published her war experiences under the name of 'Anonymous', explains why:

One had to be careful to avoid holes in the road which might have made the ambulance bump, and the slightest bump could cause a man exquisite pain.

Anonymous, WAAC: The Woman's Story of the War, 1930

Ambulance driving was heavy and tiring and it could also be dangerous work. Once when she was out driving, for example, the woman who called herself Anonymous was hit by a scrap of shell. Another night a bomb exploded only a few hundred feet in front of Beryl Hutchinson's ambulance.

There were also risks involved in working aboard hospital ships which carried the

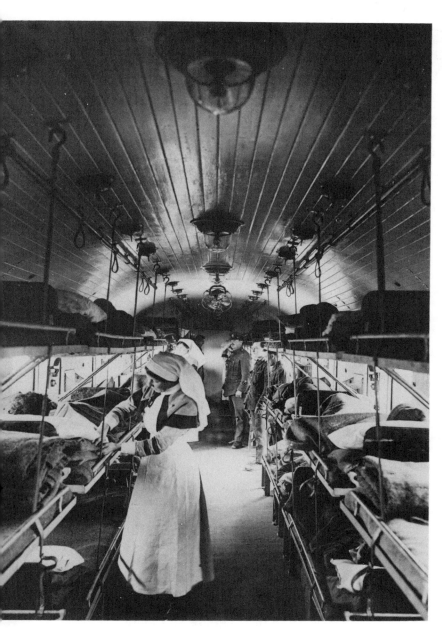

Nursing on an ambulance train. Inside a ward on a British ambulance train near Doullens, northern France, 1918.

unded home. For example, Miss Meldrum
rked as a nurse aboard a hospital ship
velling between France and England. She
s a member of the Queen Alexander
perial Military Nursing Service and
serve. During the war many ships were
k by German mines and *torpedoes*. So on
ry journey Miss Meldrum's ship was
tected:

. . . with destroyers encircling us on either side
and blue jackets [naval men] on board to keep
a lookout for mines and submarines
Letter to the Imperial War Museum, August 1919

But they were still not entirely safe and on
one of these journeys the ship was torpedoed.
Luckily Miss Meldrum was saved, although
many of the wounded men were drowned.

Pay for members of WAAC, March 1917

Occupation	Pay per week	
Ordinary clerk	23–27s	
Higher clerk	28–32s	
Shorthand typist	28–32s	
Head cook and head waitress	£40 per year	*with free board and lodgings*
Cooks, waitresses, housemaids and laundresses	£26 per year	
Superintendent, first class, of motor driving staff	52s 6d	
Superintendent, second class, of motor driving staff	46s	
Head drivers	40s	
Qualified driver mechanics	35s	
Washers	20s	
Storehouse women	20–22s	
Heading hands	22s	
Checkers	22–24s	
Assistant forewomen	24s	
Forewomen	24–30s	
Telephonists	28s	
Telegraphists	34s	
Sorters	26s	
Telephone supervisors	40s	
Telegraph supervisors	50s	
Sorters supervisors	32s	
Postwomen	20–22s	
Miscellaneous services	min. 20s	

Based on Army Council Instruction, 28 March 1917, no. 537, Employment of Women with the Armies Abroad

A large number of the women who worked at the Front belonged to and were looked after by some organisation. Members of the First Aid Nursing Yeomanry (FANYs) and the Voluntary Aid Detachment (VADs) played a very important role in helping the overworked nurses and Army Medical Corps abroad. Other organisations women could work for included the Women's Emergency Corps Canteens, the Salvation Army, the Young Women's Christian Association, the Scottish Women's Hospitals (set up by Dr Elsie Inglis) and the Women's Army Auxiliary Corps.

The *Women's Army Auxiliary Corps (WAAC)* was one of the largest organisations. It was established in February 1917 and its aim was to send women to replace men in army base camps at home and abroad. The men were then sent to the fighting line, where they were urgently needed. The WAACs were part of the armed forces and were divided into ranks. At the end of the war 9,625 women were working as WAACs abroad and 31,850 in Britain.

If you look at the table you will see both the range of jobs these women did and how much they earned. Out of their weekly wages women paid about 14s for their board and lodgings. This did not leave women who worked in the lower-paid jobs, such as postwomen and washers, with much money for themselves.

Women who worked for organisations such as the First Aid Nursing Yeomanry and the Women's Emergency Corps Canteens were not paid at all. This meant that many of the women who went to the Front were wealthy upper- and middle-class women. Working-class women could only join organisations like the WAAC, which not only paid their members but encouraged women 'from almost any class of the community' to join.

But joining the WAACs was quite complicated, as Emily Rumbold discovered. She joined in early 1917 and had to fill in an application form, send in two references, have an interview and a medical examination. Only then was she accepted. She went on a training course and was then sent to work as a storekeeper in a camp in Calais. Her work involved:

WAACs tending the graves at a war cemetery in Abbeville, northern France, September 1917. WAACs performed a vast range of important jobs at home and abroad.

Packing clothes that had been taken from dead men or wounded men and cleaned. They were being sent up the line again and we had to pack them into sacks. As one sack was filled so you passed it onto somebody else and another one was given you.

Emily Rumbold, Interview, Imperial War Museum

Emily's day was long. She had to get up at 5.30am and attend parade. She went to work at 8 or 9am and finished at 6pm. Her time was then her own but she had to be in at 9.15pm.

Ruby Ord also worked for the WAAC in Calais, as a Field Indents Clerk:

We received requests for stores from the line. They came all on a list, and we had to divide it up and send it to the various departments – depots they were called – clothing to one group, and guns, heavy guns, light guns and so forth.

Ruby Ord, Interview, Imperial War Museum

She worked longer hours than Emily Rumbold and did not finish until 8pm.

Living at the Front

The women who went to the Front, particularly women from wealthier families, did not find life easy. Living conditions were very different from what they had been used to at home. Most women found their heating and washing facilities inadequate. Rats, fleas and bugs became their frequent companions, especially at night. Food was mainly tinned rations and, as one woman recalled, 'If you weren't satisfied, that was too bad' (*Kathleen Bottomley, Interview, Imperial War Museum*).

The photograph on page 34 shows two women driving an ambulance. These women – Mairi Chisholm and Elizabeth, Baroness de T'Serclaes – were the only women to work up at the fighting line and their living conditions were very harsh. Mairi and Elizabeth worked as ambulance drivers in Belgium. They set up a dressing station 5 yards (14 metres) behind the trenches at Pervyse to care for the men from the moment they were wounded. They

33

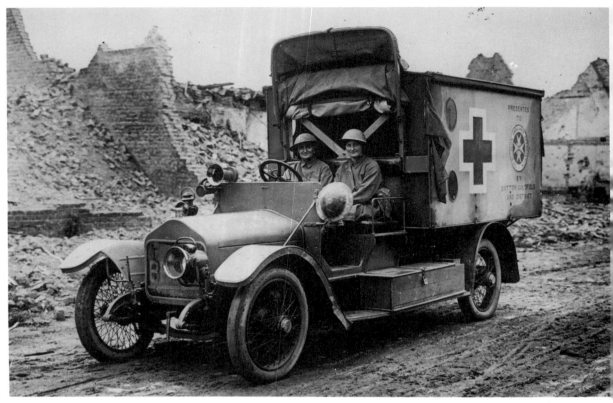

Mairi Chisholm and Elizabeth, Baroness de T'Serclaes, the 'Women of Pervyse', driving their ambulance through the ruins of Pervyse, 1917.

had to be ready to be called out at any moment:

> We slept in our clothes and cut our hair short so that it would tuck inside our caps. Dressing meant simply putting on our boots.

They were rarely able to wash:

> There were times when we had to scrape the lice off with a blunt edge of a knife and our underclothes stuck to us.
>
> *D. Mitchell (ed.), Flanders and other fields: Memoirs of the Baroness de T'Serclaes, 1964*

Mairi and Elizabeth lived in a cellar. Most other women at the Front lived in hostels, hotels, *billets* or even tents. The following description of nursing quarters in France in 1914 illustrates how difficult it was to live in a tent:

> The Sisters' Quarters was a neat compound of eight bell tents (2 to a tent), a marquee at one end and Matron's tent at the other. The kitchen consisted of a field camp oven, and a trench fire, with a temporary tarpaulin wood shed . . . We were very busy and work under these circumstances was most difficult. The tents were dark, lit only by hurricane lamps . . . The heating of the tents was by means of coke stoves made out of petrol tins with holes bored in them.
>
> *Letter from Miss Minns to the Imperial War Museum, August 1919*

Later on these tents were replaced by corrugated-iron Nissen huts. Two, eight, or even twenty women shared a hut and each hut had a cubicle for washing, and a stove in the centre.

Not only were living conditions very different from what women would have been used to at home, but women who worked in army bases and military hospitals came under

Nissen huts at the WAAC Camp No. 4 in Rouen, northern France.

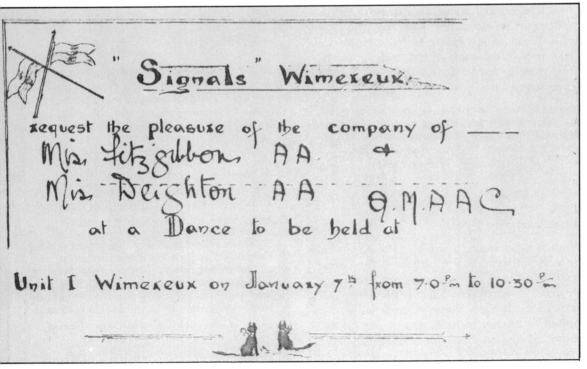

Invitation of two QMAAC members to a dance at Wimereux, northern France.

strict army discipline. There were also many rules and regulations in the other organisations.

Women were punished for being rude to officers and for slackness at work, for example, but the authorities were most concerned with how women spent their time off work. Nurses and VADs often had little free time, particularly when there had been heavy fighting at the Front Line. But when they were off-duty they were expected to go for walks or shop with one another, and not with other men. WAACs, who had more regular time off, were allowed to hold dances and invite men. But once they were off-duty, *rank and file* WAACs were strictly forbidden even to speak to male officers. However, there were ways of breaking this rule. Dolly Shepherd, a driver in the WAAC, remembers how they used to eat in hotels with male officers:

> They used to go in the front door of the hotel and get a private room and we used to go round the back door where a little boy would let us in and we used to go up that way.
>
> *Dolly Shepherd, Interview, Imperial War Museum*

Some women were not prepared to break the rule that separated women from men. Vera Brittain wrote in her autobiography about a friend called Hope Milroy. Hope was a VAD and unlike most of her colleagues she did not secretly spend time with men. Vera explains why:

> It made the men so conceited, she said, to think themselves worth any amount of risk to women who stood the chance of dismissal while they would get off scot-free whatever happened.
>
> *Vera Brittain, Testament of Youth, 1933*

Dangers at the Front

Women who went to work at the Front had to be very hardened. Not only was the work often difficult and living conditions poor, but as we have already seen their lives were sometimes in danger. Some women were wounded in enemy attacks, gassed, or taken prisoner. Many hundreds of women did not survive. They drowned when ships were sunk, died of disease or were killed in enemy raids.

IN MEMORY OF THE NOBLEST TYPE OF BRITISH WOMANHOOD.

MISS EDITH CAVELL
DIED FOR HER COUNTRY Oct. 12th 1915.

Edith Cavell: a nurse who worked for the Red Cross in German-occupied Belgium, where she cared for British, French and German soldiers. She was arrested by the Germans for helping British soldiers to escape, court-martialled, and shot on 12 October 1915. Edith Cavell became a national hero.

A bomb raid could be very frightening, as we can see from a letter written by a FANY her parents. The raid started at night and th women were told to go to the shelter:

> So down we trooped with gas masks and tin helmets on and sat there from midnight until 2 o'clock during which time the noise from the exploding shells was simply awful. The gun fired every ten minutes and no-one of course knew where the next shell was coming to.
>
> *Letter published in the Surrey Comet, August 1918*

Yet, however terrifying the raids were, mos women put their work first, as newspaper

ports showed. In an attack on a hospital in
France, for example:

The attendants utterly refused to leave the
patients but all the while the dreadful carnage
went on the nurses moved about among the
beds, smiling and doing their best to keep up
the courage of their poor charges [patients].

The Times, 24 May 1918

Similarly, in the German offensive of March
1918, the WAACs at Abbeville in northern
France were told to leave, but:

We stood firm and said we stood shoulder to
shoulder with our men and if they stayed we
did not retreat.

*Kathleen Bottomley, Interview, Imperial War
Museum*

There were raids every night and it was only
after nine WAACs were killed that they
moved into the Forest of Crécy to sleep, and
then marched into the town to do their work
during the day.

As the work involved so many dangers, why
did women go to the Front? Most women
went out of a mixture of adventure and
patriotism. The risks involved were not
thought about; women simply wanted to get to
the war. In her diary, Florence Farmborough
expresses the feelings of many women. She
trained with the Russian Red Cross, and once
she had passed her exams and was ready to set
off for the Front, she wrote:

A wild exhilaration swept like fire through my
veins, we were off, off to the Front.

*Florence Farmborough, Nurse at the Russian
Front: A Diary 1914–18, 1974*

But not all women shared Florence's support
of the war. As you will see in the next chapter
some women opposed it and tried to put an
end to it.

Nurses being presented with military medals after their hospital at Blendecques in France was bombed in 1918. Many
women received medals for their bravery during the war.

5 Fighting for peace

Most descriptions of the First World War give the impression that women whole-heartedly supported the war effort. The majority of women did support the war and earlier chapters of this book have shown how they did this by working at the Front, taking over men's jobs in offices, transport work, on the land and in factories and by collecting money for the war effort. Some women also pressurised men to go to the Front and fight.

But there was a significant minority of women who were opposed to the war. They joined peace organisations or resisted the war in their own personal way.

It is not easy to resist the war effort of one's own country, as many women found out. Opponents of the war were called traitors and were attacked at meetings. Posters advertising their meetings were pulled down, and the daily newspapers rarely mentioned the work of women peace activists as their activities were seen as a threat to national interests. This meant that it was difficult for other women to find out about peace meetings. It also makes it difficult to uncover information on the women who opposed the First World War.

The Women's International League for Permanent Peace

A unique meeting took place at the Hague in the Netherlands from 28 April to 1 May 1915. A total of 1,136 women from twelve different countries, five of which were at war, met to discuss how the war could be ended. They came from Austria, Belgium, Canada, Denmark, Germany, Great Britain, Hungary, Italy, the Netherlands, Norway, Sweden and the USA. Not only was this the first time women from different nations had ever come together during a war to show their opposition to it, but many of these women, who met as friends and sisters, came from countries which were fighting each other.

The platform at the Hague Congress, 1915. The fifth woman from the right is a British delegate, Chrystal Macmillan.

The Congress in session.

One hundred and eighty British women wanted to go to this Congress. But the government refused to give them passports, as it did not like the idea of this international women's meeting:

His Majesty's Government is of opinion that at the present moment there is much inconvenience in holding a large meeting of a political character so close to the seat of war.

Letter from the Government Permit Office, in Towards Permanent Peace: A Record of the Women's International Congress, 1915

However, three British women did manage to go to the meeting. Chrystal Macmillan and Kathleen Courtney, who were both prominent *suffragists*, had left for the Hague early to help with the organising. Emmeline Pethick Lawrence, a prominent campaigner for votes for women who had been in the United States giving lectures on women's suffrage, travelled with the 47 American delegates.

The women at the Congress set up an international organisation called the *Women's International League for Permanent Peace.* They passed twenty forceful *resolutions*, which

included demands for an immediate and permanent peace; proposals for peace education in schools; and demands for the vote for women. We can see from the final resolution how determined the women were to end the war. They decided to send 'peace' messengers (or envoys) to the governments of the countries at war and to the neutral countries, including the United States:

. . . to urge the Governments of the world to put an end to this bloodshed and to establish a just and lasting peace.

Towards Permanent Peace, 1915

Thirty-five separate visits to heads of State were made, and one of the envoys was Chrystal Macmillan from Britain.

Other women at the Congress returned home to set up national branches of the Women's International League (WIL) in their own countries. Many women who supported the WIL were upper- and middle-class women, based in London and Manchester. Helena Swanwick chaired the British branch of the International League; Margaret Ashton,

Chrystal Macmillan: one of the three British delegates at the Congress in the Hague. Afterwards she was sent as a peace envoy to urge national leaders to end the war.

Kathleen Courtney: another British delegate to reach the Hague. She became one of the vice chairwomen of the Women's International League in Britain.

Kathleen Courtney and Maude Royden were the vice chairwomen; Emmeline Pethick Lawrence became the Treasurer; and Catherine Marshall was the Honorary Secretary. By the end of 1916 the branch had 2,458 members. They published anti-war pamphlets and leaflets and held meetings. But these women soon discovered that it was not easy to organise against the war:

> These meetings are very rarely reported, owing to the press boycott, and a section of the London press has succeeded in mobilising a small gang of roughs who are prepared to spoil meetings . . . and who occasionally penetrate to the provinces.
>
> *British Section of the Women's International League for Permanent Peace, First Annual Report, 1916*

However, they did not let this hostility discourage them and by the end of the war their membership had almost doubled.

The Women's Peace Crusade

By 1916 a few women were wanting to do more than distribute anti-war leaflets and pamphlets. They wanted to go out onto the streets to show their opposition to the war. So in June 1916, the *Women's Peace Crusade* was formed. The movement appealed to a wider range of women than the WIL, and drew on some working-class support. Its aim was to organise huge anti-war demonstrations, and on 23 July 1916 the Crusade held its first demonstration in Glasgow.

'Spades not Guns', 'Plenty of Sugar', and 'No more War'.

Why did so many women attend the demonstrations? There were many different reasons. Some women had opposed the war since August 1914 seeing it as a war between governments, and not a war between ordinary people. Others condemned it because companies and individuals were using the war to make vast 'war profits', and exploit working people. Sylvia Pankhurst, well-known for her campaigns for women's suffrage, was particularly active in opposing the war for these reasons. Other women believed that it was wrong to kill, whatever the reason. But many had simply had enough of the war, with its food shortages and high prices, conscription, and the death and maiming of so many young men. Many women who supported the Women's Peace Crusade were soldiers' wives and mothers. This newspaper report illustrates the kind of letters that were pouring into the Crusade's financial appeal:

One woman, enclosing £10, says 'I have lost one son in the war, and another is in the trenches. Thank God that at last the women are waking up.'
Four soldiers wives clubbed together to send 10s saying they have not known peace of mind since the ghastly slaughter started.
Labour Leader [the weekly newspaper of the Independent Labour Party], 5 July 1917

Charlotte Despard: from February 1918 she dedicated all her time to working for the Women's Peace Crusade.

It was during the following year that the Women's Peace Crusade really got off the ground. Huge outdoor meetings were held throughout the summer of 1917 in towns and cities such as Chester, Glasgow, Leicester, Manchester and Nelson in Lancashire. Thousands of people went on the demonstrations. Women Peace Crusaders also distributed tens of thousands of anti-war leaflets. They sold thousands of Women Peace Crusade buttons with a design in white and blue, representing the Angel of Peace protecting children. And they went from house to house talking to women who could not attend meetings. Even children went on demonstrations marching through towns carrying banners saying, 'I want my Daddy',

Like the Women's International League, the Women's Peace Crusade met with hostility. Local newspapers would rarely advertise meetings and demonstrations unless it was to encourage trouble at them. Police sometimes banned demonstrations. Others were broken up by violence. This happened in Consett, Durham, in October 1917:

The principal speaker was to have been Mrs Philip Snowden, but when the chairman announced the opening hymn a large audience, chiefly of women, broke into patriotic songs. Soon afterwards the crowd rushed the platform and tore down the peace mottoes. Free fights followed and it was with great difficulty that Mrs Snowden and her supporters escaped from the building.
The Times, 31 October 1917

Despite such hostility, by the end of the war there were more than 120 branches of the Women's Peace Crusade, with thousands of women and men supporting the Crusade.

No Conscription Fellowship

As well as organising on their own, women also worked with men in other organisations and political parties which opposed the war. These included the *Independent Labour Party*, the *Union of Democratic Control* and the *No Conscription Fellowship*.

The No Conscription Fellowship was set up in 1914. At this stage of the war all the men who fought were volunteers. However, some people feared that the government would introduce *conscription*. This would make it compulsory for men to fight in the war. The No Conscription Fellowship was formed to oppose this, but the government still introduced conscription in January 1916. Local branches of the No Conscription Fellowship were set up all over the country to support men who refused to fight. These men who did refuse could appeal to a tribunal as *Conscientious Objectors*.

As many of the Conscientious Objectors were arrested and imprisoned, women took over the running of the Fellowship. Lydia Smith, a teacher from Brighton, began editing the No Conscription Fellowship's journal, *The Tribunal*. The government banned the journal so it had to be edited in secret. Violet Tillard ran the maintenance fund, which gave financial support to families of imprisoned Conscientious Objectors. Catherine Marshall, of the Women's International League, became the Fellowship's Acting Honorary Secretary. She kept a record of every Conscientious Objector; this numbered about 16,000. She helped find paid work for the 200 men who managed to avoid arrest. And in May 1916, she organised a watch on railway stations to see that Conscientious Objectors were not taken to France to be shot as *deserters*.

Many other women worked for local branches of the No Conscription Fellowship. One woman, Helen Pease, was the acting secretary in Stoke. She used to go to the special court hearings (tribunals) of the Conscientious Objectors, find out where the men were taken if they were imprisoned, and help their families. She also used to smuggle information in and out of prison to Conscientious Objectors:

> I used to write out these reports, type them on very fine paper. And I remember I sent him [George Howell] . . . a prayer book, I think it was, or bible, some devotional work, with it pasted in the two back pages and a letter purporting to come from a very pious aunt . . . And another time I folded the paper and put it in the cuff lining of a shirt.
>
> *Helen Pease, Interview, Imperial War Museum*

Individual acts of resistance

Some individuals who did not belong to organisations also resisted the war effort.

As we have already seen, about 200 Conscientious Objectors escaped arrest. This was only possible with the help of women.

Rosa Hobhouse: she wrote many letters to bishops and MPs, reminding them of Christian pacifist beliefs.

riends and relatives hid Conscientious
Objectors in their homes. If they had been
caught both the women and the Conscientious
Objectors would have been imprisoned.
Because the women had to operate in secret, it
is difficult to find out anything about the
hiding of Conscientious Objectors. Fortunately
Sylvia Pankhurst recorded one instance in her
autobiography of the war years. You can see
in the quotation that Sylvia was careful not to
mention any names:

> Mrs— one of our Bow members who had been
> in prison as a suffragette with the help of
> another member, a dressmaker living alone,
> succeeded in hiding her husband and brother-
> in-law until the war was over.
> *Sylvia Pankhurst, The Home Front, 1932*

In 1916, two women, Rosa Hobhouse and
Clara Cole, were both sentenced to three
months' imprisonment for resisting the war. In
the summer of that year Rosa and Clara set
out on foot on a peace pilgrimage through
Bedfordshire and Northamptonshire. They
distributed hundreds of anti-war leaflets. But
after only five days of their pilgrimage they
were arrested and put on trial. Rosa's aunt
wrote:

> We have been much concerned with Rosa
> Hobhouse's trial at Kettering for preaching the
> Quaker doctrines of peace in the villages –
> 'trying to create a peace atmosphere' was the
> charge most dwelt on.
> *Lady Courtney, Extracts From a War Diary,*
> *1927*

Not all women who opposed the war were
against the war from the start. For example,
Sybil Morrison became an ambulance driver
when the war began. Then, one day, a
Zeppelin was shot down above London.

Anti-German rioting: a crowd smashing the windows of a German shop in London.

Sixty people were reported to be burning alive in it. Everyone was out on the streets clapping, singing and cheering because they were the German enemy. Suddenly Sybil knew that she could no longer support the war. She remembered:

> It was like a flash to me that this was what war did; it created this utter inhumanity in perfectly decent, nice, gentle, kindly people. I can't go on with it.
>
> *Sybil Morrison, Interview, Imperial War Museum*

So she left her job as an ambulance driver and from that day always opposed war.

The war ended on 11 November 1918. Many women have continued to resist the wars of this century. New organisations have been formed, but many others are linked to women's peace activities of the First World War. The Women's International League for Permanent Peace became the Women's International League for Peace and Freedom in 1919, and it still exists today.

Armistice Day, 11 November 1918. People celebrating the end of the war outside Buckingham Palace in London.

6 Conclusion

There is not just one story to be told about women's lives during the First World War, but many. As the previous chapters show, women's experience of the war was very diverse. It depended on many factors, including their social background, occupation, age, family life and the part of Britain they came from. Women of all classes played a crucial role in the war effort by working in different occupations on the home and fighting fronts. Some women took up new occupations in factories, transport, the Land Army, the Women's Services and nursing. As many as 5,000 women went abroad to work at the front. A minority of women campaigned for an end to the war. Women had to deal with a range of different hardships such as long working hours, dangerous or difficult jobs, male opposition to what they were doing, food shortages and rising prices. Many also had to cope with the absence or death of loved ones in the war.

Although women's experiences did differ, the war undoubtedly brought about changes in all women's lives. How lasting were these changes? In some areas of women's lives the changes were permanent, in others they were temporary. For instance, most of the difficulties in domestic life – the double burden of paid work and running the home and the shortages of food – were resolved with the end of the war. When the men returned home women were expected to give up their war work and go back to their former 'female' roles and occupations.

However, many women had now tasted financial and social independence. They had made new friends and in many cases earned higher wages than before. Some women had been involved in campaigns for lower rents, for equal pay with men, for increased separation allowances, and for peace. As a result many women's self image and confidence had increased, and this could not be taken away from them. As one woman who worked during the First World War recently said:

It allowed women to stand on their own feet.

Jane Cox, Interview, Imperial War Museum

Questions

1   Give examples of the different types of evidence used in this book. Which do you consider to be the most reliable? Which do you consider to be the least reliable? Give reasons for your answers.

2   This book uses oral evidence. How useful is oral evidence to historians? Think about memory lapse, different personalities and experiences, and personal bias, when you discuss your answer. Think about how you would organise an oral interview. What preparations would you need to make? How far could the wording you use affect the results you obtain? Discuss what questions you would ask somebody about their experiences during a war.

3   Look at the leaflet, *To the Young Women of London*, on page 29. Who do you think might have circulated this leaflet? What effect do you think this leaflet might have had on women? How would you find out? How are women and men portrayed in this leaflet?

4   Look at the extract from the pamphlet, *The Underworld of Manchester in War Time*, on page 27. How would you find out if women were spending their separation allowance in public houses? Why do you think the magistrate wrote this pamphlet? What effects do you think such a pamphlet might have had on anyone who read it?

5   Look at the letter from the *Lady's Pictorial* on page 25. Why do you think women were being urged to turn their attention to the care of the young? What implications does the letter have for different groups of women e.g. women who were engaged in full-time work? Childless women?

What other sources could you look at to see if these sentiments were shared by everyone?

6   Give as many reasons as you can why women became involved in the war effort.

7   Although women took part in nearly all aspects of the war, they were not involved in the actual fighting. Why do you think this was so?

8   List the ways in which the First World War changed women's lives. Were these changes temporary or permanent?

9   Women gained the vote in 1918. Some historians believe it was the women's effort in the war that contributed to this. Try and give as many reasons as you can why this might be so. Then read any book on the suffragette movement. What new reasons might there be for women obtaining the vote?

10 Compare the jobs done by women today with those done in the war. What similarities and differences do you notice?

11 Interview a woman today about her work. Include the type of work, working conditions, rates of pay, and length of the working-day in your questioning. What has changed and what has remained the same since the First World War?

12 What were the aims of the Women's International League for Permanent Peace?
Find out about other women's initiatives to promote peace in this century.

Further reading

th Adam, *A Woman's Place 1910–75*, Chatto & Windus, 1975

ne O. Andrews, *The Economic Effects of the World War upon Women and Children*, Oxford University Press, 1921

thur Bowley, *Prices and Wages in the United Kingdom, 1914–20*, Oxford University Press, 1921

il Braybon, *Women Workers in the First World War: The British Experience*, Croom Helm, 1981

Braybon and Penny Summerfield, *Out of the Cage: Women's Experiences in the Two World Wars*, Pandora, 1987

ra Brittain, *Testament of Youth. An Autobiographical Study of the Years 1900–25*, Victor Gollancz, 1933

E. Bulkley, *A Bibliographical Survey of Contemporary Sources for the Economic and Social History of the War*, Oxford University Press, 1922

rtrude Bussey and Margaret Timms, *Pioneers for Peace: Women's International League for Peace and Freedom 1915–65*, Allen & Unwin, 1965

ne Clephane, *Towards Sex Freedom*, John Lane, 1935

vid Englander, *Landlord and Tenant in Urban Britain, 1838–1918*, Oxford University Press, 1983

rence Farmborough, *Nurse at the Russian Front: A Diary 1914–18*, Constable, 1974

llicent Garrett Fawcett, *The Women's Victory and After: Personal Reminiscences 1911–18*, Sidgwick and Jackson, 1920

te Haste, *Keep the Home Fires Burning: Propaganda in the First World War*, Allen Lane, 1977

A. W. Kirkaldy, *British Labour, Replacement and Conciliation, 1914–21*, Pitman & Sons, 1921

Arthur Marwick, *The Deluge: British Society and the First World War*, Macmillan, 1965

Arthur Marwick, *Women at War 1914–18*, Fontana, 1977

David Mitchell, *Women on the Warpath: The Story of Women in the First World War*, Jonathan Cape, 1965

Sylvia Pankhurst, *The Home Front*, Hutchinson, 1932

C. S. Peel, *How We Lived Then, 1914–18*, John Lane, 1929

Emmeline Pethick Lawrence, *My Part in a Changing World*, Victor Gollancz, 1938

Catherine Reilly (ed.), *Scars upon my Heart: Women's Poetry and Verse of the First World War*, Virago, 1981

Sheila Rowbotham, *Hidden From History: 300 Years of Women's Oppression and the Fight against it*, Pluto, 1973

Arthur Shadwell, *Drink in 1914–22: A Lesson in Control*, Longman Green, 1923

A. J. P. Taylor, *The First World War: An Illustrated History*, Penguin, 1966

Trevor Wilson, *The Myriad Faces of War*, Polity, 1986

Anne Wiltsher, *Most Dangerous Women: Feminist Peace Campaigners of the Great War*, Pandora, 1985

Jay Winter, *The Great War and the British People*, Macmillan, 1986

L. K. Yates, *A Woman's Part: A Record of Munitions Work*, Hodder and Stoughton, 1918

Glossary

billet accommodation for soldiers etc. with the local population

chaperone an older (often married) woman who accompanies a younger, unmarried woman on social occasions

conscription compulsory joining of the armed forces

Conscientious Objector someone who refuses to do something on grounds of their conscience (their beliefs)

demobilise to disband (dismiss) troops

deserter someone who runs away from service in the armed forces

enlist join the army

First Aid Nursing Yeomanry organisation started in 1909. Its aim was to assist the Royal Army Medical Corps in time of war by providing horse waggon ambulances to transport the wounded. Members, known as FANYs, were unpaid volunteers

Independent Labour Party socialist party formed in 1893. It opposed the First World War, unlike the Labour Party

munitions military weapons, ammunition, equipment and stores

No Conscription Fellowship organisation set up in 1914 to oppose compulsory conscription for men

rank and file ordinary members of an organisation, rather than the leaders

rations a fixed amount of food and coal that people were allowed to buy each week

resolutions agreements for the future

séance spiritualist activity with the aim of making contact with the dead

suffragist someone who campaigned for votes for women, using non-violent methods

torpedo underwater missile that can be aimed at a ship, and explodes on hitting it

Union of Democratic Control organisation founded in August 1914. It aimed to restore parliamentary control of foreign policy

Venereal Disease (VD) contagious disease such as syphilis or gonorrhoea, spread by sexual intercourse

Voluntary Aid Detachment organisation set up in 1910. It aimed to provide help for the sick and wounded in case of an enemy invasion. Members, known as VADs, were volunteers and during the war were paid a small weekly sum (equivalent of £20 a year)

war bonus money paid to many workers to cover the increase in the cost of living during the war. Men were usually given a higher bonus than women

Women's Army Auxiliary Corps (WAAC) organisation begun in 1917 to send women to replace men in Army base camps, so that the men could be sent to fight at the Front

Women's Co-operative Guild organisation begun in 1883. Its aim was to encourage women's interest in the co-operative movement. By 1914 it had about 30,000 members, mostly working-class. During the war the Guild used every opportunity to push for improvements in the position of working-class women

Women's Freedom League organisation formed in 1907 to campaign for votes for women

Women's International League for Permanent Peace international organisation set up in 1915 to promote immediate and permanent peace. In 1919 it changed its name to the Women's International League for Peace and Freedom, and it continues its work today

Women's Peace Crusade organisation formed in 1916 to oppose the war through demonstrations

Zeppelin a cylindrical-shaped airship. From around 1900 Zeppelins were used to carry passengers, and during the war they were used for reconnaissance and bombing